# Socially Responsible Investing

## Aligning Values and Wealth Creation

# Table of Contents

# Chapter 1. Introduction

Welcome to a groundbreaking and heartening Special Report that bridges fiscal pragmatism with ethical significance - "Socially Responsible Investing: Aligning Values and Wealth Creation." This special edition underscores how you can harmonize your financial objectives with your core ethics, carving a path to prosperity that doesn't compromise your deepest-held values. Dive into this stimulating read peppered with exclusive interviews, case studies, and strategies articulated by experts, demonstrating how socially responsible investing can create meaningful impact while strengthening your financial position. If you have ever pondered about making your money work in a way that resonates with your ethos, this report is your compass. It's not just about enriching your financial knowledge; it's about enriching your life and the world around you. Let's step into the future of investing – ethically and lucratively.

# Chapter 2. Understanding Socially Responsible Investing

Socially responsible investing (SRI) is not a newfangled concept, but its importance has been amplified in today's interconnected and enlightened world, where businesses shape societies and economies influence ecosystems. Sparing from the cliché of simply doing well by doing good, SRI intertwines the threads of sustainable fiscal gains with the fabric of ethical consciousness.

## 2.1. Unraveling the Concept

SRI operates under the premise that corporations involved in socially and environmentally sustainable practices are likely to be more resilient and potentially more profitable in the long run. It's a way to invest in companies that mirror your own values, without necessarily sacrificing potential returns. Investors adhering to SRI often evaluate potential investments based on both financial return and social good.

The philosophies underpinning SRI are twofold: First, companies that behave responsibly pertaining to societal and environmental issues may reap reputational benefits, driving consumer demand and potentially increasing profitability. Second, companies that ignore these factors may face material risks due to regulatory, reputational, and operational challenges.

## 2.2. The Many Faces of Socially Responsible Investing

Much like traditional investing, SRI can be approached via various forms: stock investing, bonds investment, private equity, mutual funds, and exchange-traded funds (ETFs).

When investing in stocks or equity, the SRI investor would consider the company's operational practices, its products and services, and its engagement with the community. For example, they may prefer companies with strong records in environmental stewardship, stakeholder relations, and labor practices.

Bond investors adopting SRI might focus on green bonds, which fund projects with an environmental benefit, or social bonds that aim at positive socio-economic outcomes.

Private equity in the realm of SRI could mean investing in start-ups and private companies focusing on green technologies or those addressing social issues, like affordable housing or financial inclusion.

SRI mutual funds and ETFs provide an efficient way for investors to access a diversified portfolio of socially responsible investments.

## 2.3. Measuring Social Impact: ESG Factors

As an investor, how do you determine if a company is socially responsible or not? That's where ESG factors come into play. ESG stands for Environmental, Social, and Governance, three key metrics used to evaluate a company's impact on the world.

The 'E' in ESG refers to a company's environmental

responsibilities—how it deals with issues like climate change, deforestation, water scarcity, pollution, and waste management.

'S' stands for social responsibilities, looking at how the company treats its employees, suppliers, customers, and the communities where it operates. This includes the company's labor standards, human rights policies, health and safety protocols, and diversity practices.

The 'G' in ESG stands for governance, evaluating how a company is managed. This includes factors such as executive compensation, board diversity, corporate ethics, and shareholder rights.

## 2.4. The Impact of Socially Responsible Investing

SRI allows you to align your investments with your values and make a meaningful impact. By choosing to invest in companies that meet high ESG standards, you're indirectly encouraging corporations to act responsibly, ethically, and sustainably. Consequently, these companies are incentivized to improve their practices to attract investment.

Besides contributing to social change, SRI also brings about positive financial repercussions. A growing body of research suggests that investments adhering to ESG standards are just as likely, if not more likely, to perform well compared to traditional investments. Therefore, SRI can form a core part of your investment strategy, potentially adding diversification and defensibility while contributing to the causes you care about.

In conclusion, socially responsible investing is about sincere participation in the tapestry of societal development, etching your values in the fabric of economic progress. It's a twofold journey, leading you to robust financial growth while kindling a positive societal transformation. It's not only good business; it is wholesome participation in a global tribe of conscious citizens creating a more equitable, humane, and sustainable world. For someone looking to join the ranks of such ethical investors, the following chapters will serve as an informative guide on how to commence and navigate this rewarding journey.

# Chapter 3. The Inner Mechanics of Ethical Wealth Generation

The march toward attaining monetary gains while sustaining cherished beliefs starts with an unequivocal understanding of the underlying concepts. It's a multilayered journey - a blend of financial acumen, societal consciousness, and a willing heart to make a difference.

## 3.1. Instrument Selection and its Implications

Identifying the right investment assets is a cornerstone of ethical wealth generation. Various instruments enable wealth creation while aligning with ethical concerns. Equity shares of 'green' companies, bonds floated by non-profits, or mutual funds with ESG (Environmental, Social, Governance) considerations – these can be some avenues your investment car can traverse. Investment in green bonds, for instance, is often directed toward projects that address climate change, while ESG-focused funds prefer companies that adhere to ethical practices.

Moreover, it is crucial to screen assets beyond the 'green' tag. Detailed analysis of a company's operations, its impact on stakeholders, policies addressing ethical concerns, commitment to sustainability, and overall performance in ESG metrics are incredibly important. Tools like MSCI ESG ratings can facilitate this necessary diligence.

# 3.2. Creating an Ethical Portfolio

Crafting a portfolio goes beyond pooling individually ethical assets. An effective portfolio embodies balance and diversification, safeguarding your investments from market volatility while ensuring consistent returns. But how does one create a diversified ethical portfolio? The answer lies in a strategy that revolves around ESG parameters.

Consider a hypothetical situation: You have a 50/50 equities/bonds portfolio, consisting of shares from renewable-energy companies and bonds issued by nonprofits, respectively. Now, imagine if market dynamics turn against renewable energy businesses. The 50 % equity portion could suffer a considerable hit. A more resilient strategy could involve diversifying within each asset class.

Agency bonds, green bonds, municipal bonds, ESG-focused bond funds could form your bond pool, whereas the equities could have brands from varied sectors like waste management, renewable energy, healthcare - all selected for their high ESG ratings.

# 3.3. Aligning Values with Profit

The next facet of ethical wealth generation circles back to the basics of investing - profitability. Being ethical doesn't mean compromising on financial wealth. Rather, it implies making one's money work in a way that resonates with their values, upholds ethics, and caters to financial goals.

Studies affirm that companies fulfilling their social and environmental responsibilities witness strong customer loyalty, reducing business risk. Also, ESG-oriented companies generally follow a robust governance structure, further driving profitability. Therefore, aligning your values with your investments can lead to fruitful wealth generation, setting up a virtuous cycle of positive societal impact and financial gains.

## 3.4. The Role of Philanthropy

Contributing to charitable causes – another dimension of ethical wealth generation – nurtures societal betterment and nourishes one's inner ethos. This needn't be 'giving away' wealth; indeed, philanthropy can be a strategic approach, utilizing different vehicles to create a broader impact while yielding monetary benefits.

One could establish a trust, fund a scholarship, or create a foundation, leading to substantial societal improvements and probable tax benefits. Additionally, one may consider 'impact investing' - investing in social enterprises that strive to generate societal benefits alongside financial returns.

## 3.5. Conclusion

To maneuver the labyrinth of ethical wealth generation, a meticulous understanding of specialized instruments, a meticulously crafted portfolio, an unwavering focus on ESG values without sacrificing profits, and a strategic approach toward philanthropy is seminal. In conclusion, ethical wealth generation implies giving your wealth a purpose – a purpose that resonates with your core beliefs, nurtures societal welfare, and cultivates a prosperous future. Such an approach does not merely spell success from a financial perspective; it fosters inner satisfaction, fostering a legacy that outlasts one's life.

# Chapter 4. The Shift towards Conscious Capital: Historical Insights

The evolution of socially responsible investing (SRI) has been a slow, but rewarding journey of financial awakening and ethical enlightenment. Spread over decades, this shift is historically significant, as it presents a nuanced picture of how integral societal values have come to be intertwined with investment decisions.

## 4.1. The Early Seeds of Conscious Capital

The origin story of SRI dates back to the religious communities of the 18th century. The Quakers, Mennonites, and Methodists were among the pioneering communities that practiced nascent forms of SRI. These groups discouraged their members from participating in ventures that were inconsistent with their religious beliefs, such as slavery, alcohol, gambling, and military-related businesses. This was a strikingly important stride in linking faith with financial decisions and thus exhibiting a precursory form of SRI.

## 4.2. The Awakening in the 20th Century

Fast forward to the 20th century, during the volatile 1960s, SRI started to manifest as an organized movement. The Civil Rights Movement, the Vietnam War, and the ensuing peace campaign played a pivotal role in shaping the SRI movement in its early stages. The war led investors to scrutinize defense-related investments, and the Civil Rights Movement propelled efforts for workplace diversity and equal employment opportunity. Such considerations birthed an investment paradigm that was not only about financial gain but also about ethical impact.

## 4.3. The Genesis of Organized SRI

The 1970s marked the creation of professionally managed SRI funds. The Pax World Fund, launched in 1971, was the first such mutual fund to screen out companies involved in manufacturing weapons for warfare, thus setting the stage for SRI's modern form. This period also witnessed the genesis of shareholder activism, through which investors began to voice concerns over corporate policies and practices.

SRI funds grew steadily in the 1980s, bolstered by the anti-apartheid movement which led to the divestment of companies doing business in South Africa. This was one of the most prominent examples of investors exerting influence to address a pressing social issue.

## 4.4. The Emergence of ESG

As the millennium dawned, the concept of ESG (Environmental, Social, and Governance) criteria emerged, proliferating across the investment landscape. ESG investing entails assessing companies based on their environmental impact, societal contributions, and governance structures. It reflected a nuanced understanding of SRI, emphasizing that companies with sustainable practices often tend to yield better long-term performances.

The 2006 United Nations-backed Principles for Responsible Investment Initiative (UNPRI) served as a global milestone in urging the incorporation of ESG factors into investment analysis. Today, ESG investing has become a staple in many investment portfolios, underscoring the far-reaching consequences of the shift towards conscious capitalism.

# 4.5. Exploring Ethical Indices and Corporate Sustainability Reports

Following the surge of ESG, ethical indices like the Dow Jones Sustainability Indices (DJSI) and FTSE4Good were launched, providing a gateway for investors to monitor the sustainability performance of companies. Moreover, the advent of corporate sustainability reports empowered investors with detailed narratives of companies' ESG performances, enabling a profound shift towards transparency and accountability.

# 4.6. Perspective: Transformations in Investment Philosophy

The historical evolution of SRI has seen subtle shifts in the way investments are perceived. What began as a crusade against unethical businesses has morphed into proactive support for companies fulfilling ESG criteria. Investors are no longer considering just how to avoid harm, but also how to contribute positively to society. This reflects a marked transition from negative screening to positive screening in investment decisions.

# 4.7. Investment Landscape: Into the Future

As we venture further into the 21st century, the seismic shift towards SRI and ESG is set to continue. New and emerging themes such as impact investing, green bonds, and sustainable development goals (SDGs) are framing the future of conscious capital.

In sum, the historical trajectory of SRI reveals the gradual, yet tenacious, integration of ethical values into the world of finance. The increasing convergence of profits with purpose conveys a hopeful message: conscious capital isn't a utopian dream but an achievable and lucrative reality. This journey towards conscious capital is indeed a testament to our collective capacity to transmute economic goals into ethical triumphs, to blend prudential investing with principled living, and to design a more inclusive, sustainable, and equitable financial landscape.

# Chapter 5. Analyzing Profitability of Socially Responsible Investments

Investors often wrestle with the hypothesis if ethical considerations align with financial gains. Socially Responsible Investments (SRIs) challenge this narrative by redefining the traditional investment paradigm. The essence lies in thoughtful selection- investments that are profitable and simultaneously bring about positive societal impact. This intriguing balance kindles a pertinent question - how does one gauge the profitability of SRIs?

## 5.1. Establishing Understanding: What is Socially Responsible Investing?

Socially Responsible Investing, often denoted as SRI or ESG (Environmental, Social, Governance) Investing, embeds ethical considerations within financial decisions. Fundamentally, it entails investments into businesses that adhere to sustainable practices that benefit our society or environment. SRIs may encompass myriad fields, ranging from clean energy initiatives to enterprises working for social equity, corporate governance, or the welfare of employees.

SRI signifies not an isolated concept but rather an investment methodology that merges traditional financial analysis and risk correction with ethical accountability. This dual-purpose makes SRIs hugely attractive; however, it also implies an additional layer to the conventional profitability analysis.

## 5.2. Decoding the Profitability Aspect

Profitability is a measure of a company's potential to yield returns on investment. Analysis of this key factor includes evaluating revenue and net income growth, understanding profit margins, and examining Cash Flow Statements.

Revenue Growth indicates an increase in a company's sales over a given period. A rising trend shows a thriving business, potentially reflecting its popularity or superior product offerings.

Net Income Growth is indicative of the surplus generated post accounting for all overheads, including operational expenses, taxation, and the like. It's crucial as it reflects the actual profit which will be potentially paid out to stakeholders or retained for future growth.

Profit Margins illustrate the proportion of income retained post cost incurrence. High profit margins typically indicate better cost control and productivity.

Cash Flow Statements inspect the cash movements in and out of a firm. Cash inflow mainly comes from primary business operations, but it also includes investments and financing.

But profitability in the context of SRIs also includes considering the company's ESG factors. High ESG scores directly correlate with adhering to a wider range of stakeholders' interests. These may translate into lower risk and, potentially, better long-term returns.

# 5.3. Unraveling Financial Performances of SRIs

A multitude of academic and financial pieces of research suggest that SRIs don't necessarily imply less profitability. Some studies establish a positive correlation between strong ESG practices and financial performances; others claim a neutral effect while only a few present negative outcomes. Below are the key sermons from an array of studies:

1. A 2015 report by the Deutsche Bank indicated that companies with high ESG scores had a lower cost of capital, lower volatility, and fewer instances of corporate fraud.

2. The study, "ESG and financial performance: aggregated evidence from more than 2000 empirical studies," clarifies that the majority of the research finds a nonnegative relation between ESG measures and corporate financial performance.

Investors, therefore, shouldn't falsely equate SRIs with impaired profitability.

# 5.4. Exploring Diverse Sectors: Examples of Profitable SRIs

Profitable SRIs are pervasive across industries. For instance, NextEra Energy Inc., an SRI in the renewable energy landscape, has witnessed significant revenue growth over the past years, making it a profitable venture. Another example is Unilever, which has committed to its sustainable living plan, driving profitability and social good simultaneously.

# 5.5. Conclusion: Navigating the Way

Analyzing the profitability of Socially Responsible Investments is intrinsically linked to the fusion of sound financial analysis and detailed ESG evaluation. Knowledge, patience, and holistic evaluation of both financial and ESG metrics compose the road to profitable SRI decisions.

Investing does not signify a binary choice between wealth creation and bearing social responsibility. Rather, it's about striking a balance, transforming the investing landscape into a platform that promotes sustainability, corporate ethics, and financial success in harmony. Thus, responsible profitability is not only achievable, but it ennobles the spirit of investing itself.

In the end, it's no longer about "Can we afford to invest ethically?" but "Can we afford not to?"

# Chapter 6. Key Players in the Field of Social Responsibility Investment

In the burgeoning landscape of Social Responsibility Investment (SRI), certain key players have emerged as torchbearers. These entities are shaking up the investment world by combining smart business acumen with an unwavering commitment to ethical decision-making. This chapter takes a detailed look at such transformative influencers, studying their operational mechanisms, accomplishments, and the profound influence they have on the global investment community.

## 6.1. Investment Funds Focused on Ethical Investments

In the realm of SRI, several dedicated funds have been trailblazers in the area of ethical investments. Among these, Calvert Impact Capital, Domini Impact Investments, and Trillium Asset Management have carved significant niches in the sector.

Calvert Impact Capital, a non-profit investment firm, serves as an impressive example of a devoted SRI fund. The firm works on leveraging capital from different sources and directing it towards burgeoning enterprises worldwide that pledge to create a positive social and environmental impact.

Domini Impact Investments is another leader that has built a rich portfolio of ethically-sound investments. The firm scrutinizes potential investments using rigorous standards that evaluate the social and environmental implications of each business operation. As of 2020, Domini managed around $2.5 billion in assets across its various mutual funds.

Meanwhile, Trillium Asset Management, one of the oldest investment firms in the SRI field, has the distinction of being the first US-based firm to manage environmentally-focused investment portfolios. With ESG integration at the core, Trillium makes a compelling case for profitability aligning with social responsibility.

## 6.2. The Role of International Organizations

International bodies, such as the United Nations and the World Bank, have also played a significant role in scaling SRI. Their programs and initiatives have been instrumental in fostering improved business ethics and advocating for sustainable development.

The United Nations spearheaded the Principles for Responsible Investment (PRI) in 2006 along with an international network of investors. Today, over 3,000 signatories manage investing in accordance with the six principles that underline environmental, social, and governance (ESG) factors in investment decision-making and ownership practices.

The World Bank has been another major influence in making sustainable businesses a priority. The bank's International Finance Corporation (IFC) launched its Sustainable Bond Program to attract investors who wish to support projects that seek to mitigate climate change and encourage sustainable growth in developing nations.

## 6.3. Corporate Social Responsibility Initiatives

Corporate-led initiatives are another crucial component of the SRI ecosystem. Companies across various industries have started to prioritize religiously their responsibilities towards the society and environment.

Google, for instance, has committed to operate entirely on renewable energy. Similarly, Patagonia, an outdoor clothing company, has pledged 1% of its total sales or 10% of its profit—whichever is more—to environmental groups. Unilever, under the Unilever Sustainable Living Plan, is another corporate that aims to halve the environmental impact of its products by 2030.

Corporate Social Responsibility (CSR) initiatives like these indicate a shift in how businesses view their roles, evolving from meagre profit-makers to entities capable of driving significant social change.

## 6.4. Impact of Financial Institutions

Banks and financial institutions also hold enormous sway in shaping the realm of SRI. By creatively leveraging their resources and aligning their services with SRI commitments, these institutions tap into the growing demand for ethical investments.

In 2016, Goldman Sachs bought Imprint Capital, an impact investing firm, marking an unprecedented move by a major bank into the SRI field. Meanwhile, Credit Suisse, Barclays, BNP Paribas, and others have set up dedicated SRI and impact investing teams, signaling the rising importance of SRI in mainstream finance.

## 6.5. Role of Regulatory Bodies

Lastly, regulatory bodies have the power to significantly steer the direction and scope of SRI. The regulatory frameworks they initiate can encourage or discourage ethical investing. An example is the European Union (EU), which has prioritized sustainable finance through various legislation, setting a global standard for other nations to follow.

While the key players in the field of Social Responsibility Investment are diverse, their shared vision for a profitable yet ethical financial ecosystem unites them. As stakeholders in what promises to transform traditional investing, each plays a unique role in establishing a future where capital is not just about profit, but people and the planet as well. The collective actions of these entities are accelerating the shift towards SRI, creating an investment landscape congruent with the growing societal recognition of sustainability — a necessity for our shared future.

# Chapter 7. Strategies for Successful Socially Responsible Investing

Investing has traditionally been driven simply by profit. However, a paradigm shift is occurring; one where money-making and moral compass are not mutually exclusive domains. Achieving this delicate balancing of fiscal growth and ethical impact involves a carefully curated strategy and approach.

## 7.1. Understanding Socially Responsible Investing (SRI)

Before diving into strategies, it's important to sketch a solid context around Socially Responsible Investing (SRI). At its core, SRI means leveraging your financial potential to create substantial societal change without implicating your financial returns.

SRI constitutes three main dimensions - Environmental, Social, and Governance factors (ESG). Companies ranked higher on ESG are generally more conscientious about their impact and are likely to be safer investments as they navigate various socio-political, environmental, and regulatory challenges.

## 7.2. The Power of Screening

One overarching strategy for SRI is screening. Before investing, evaluate potential firms using two key screening tactics: positive or negative screening.

Positive screening involves selecting companies that proactively foster environmental welfare, encourage societal development, and maintain a high degree of corporate governance. Meanwhile, negative screening implies eliminating companies from your investment list that engage in harmful activities, such as animal cruelty or fossil fuel reliance.

*caption: Positive and Negative Screening*

To maximize the efficiency of this technique, utilize credible ESG rating agencies like MSCI and Sustainalytics. Their data-rich insights can guide your investment decisions, aligning with both wealth creation and social responsibility.

## 7.3. Impact Investing: Addressing Social Issues

For investors looking to catalyze substantial change, impact investing is a sterling approach. This strategy involves investing directly in causes or organizations with a measurable, constructive societal or environmental outcome, along with a financial return.

Remember that impact investing mandates thorough due diligence – both on the organization's financial prospects and their ability to craft a substantial impact.

*Table 1. Table: Top sectors for Impact Investing (Global Impact Investing Network)*

| Education | Health | Agriculture | Renewable energy |
| --- | --- | --- | --- |

## 7.4. Green Bonds: Financing Sustainable Projects

Green bonds are rapidly becoming a preferred option for SRI. These fixed-income investments finance environmentally friendly projects, helping corporations and governments shift towards greener alternatives. Investing in green bonds allows you to be a part of these transformative initiatives, aligning your wealth creation with tackling climate change.

## 7.5. Community Investing: Boosting Local Economies

A unique and fulfilling approach to SRI is community investing. By investing in local businesses, low-income housing initiatives, or community development banks, you become an active participant in nurturing your local economy. Not only does this generate financial returns, but it also weaves a fabric of prosperity and resilience at the community level.

Community investing, however, requires intimate knowledge of the local domain and demands patience, given the time it can take to realize financial return.

## 7.6. Active Ownership: Influence Corporate Policies

Another empowering strategy for SRI is active ownership. As an active owner, you can use your voice to shape corporate decisions via voting rights and engagement initiatives. You can advocate for better ESG practices, endorse diversity, and push for transparency, strengthening the company's long-term sustainability and consequently, your investment.

## 7.7. Following Industry Trends

A dynamic approach to SRI involves staying alert to sustainability trends as pathways to optimize your investments. This could mean investing in industries like renewable energy, which are expected to flourish in the coming decade, or divesting from companies that fail to align with future sustainability norms.

## 7.8. Diversification of Portfolio

*By observing trends, you not only align yourself with the future of business but also place yourself at the forefront of wealth creation and delivering social impact.*

While SRI is about impact, prudent investing principles still hold. Having a diverse portfolio can safeguard your investments from market volatilities. Consider varying your investments across sectors, geographical regions, and financial products that match your SRI criteria.

## 7.9. Engaging a Specialist

Finally, given the nuanced nature of SRI, engaging a financial advisor who specializes in this zone could be beneficial. They can guide you through the process, helping you navigate the landscape of SRI opportunities and steer towards your twin goals of financial and ethical success.

To conclude, socially responsible investing is a journey. It's about finding the right balance between your financial goals and ethical considerations. It's about making informed decisions to make a difference - one portfolio at a time. Let's reimagine investing - not just as a wealth creation strategy, but as a tool to shape a more sustainable world.

# Chapter 8. Challenges in Socially Responsible Investing: Mitigation Techniques

Socially responsible investing (SRI), while increasingly recognised for its multifaceted benefits, is not without its unique set of challenges. A nuanced understanding of these can empower investors to navigate potential obstacles, thereby enhancing the likelihood of achieving both their ethical and financial goals.

## 8.1. Understanding SRI Landscapes and Terminologies

The realm of SRI is replete with a myriad of terminologies such as Environmental, Social and Governance (ESG), sustainable investing, impact investing, and ethical investing. This proliferation of terms can sometimes be dizzying, creating a hurdle for investors aiming to understand and navigate this ever-expanding domain.

Furthermore, defining and measuring social responsibility can be demanding. What constitutes a 'socially responsible' company might hinge upon individual investors' ethical norms and values. For instance, one investor might focus on companies with strong environmental stewardship, while another could concentrate on those that prioritise gender equality or employ fair trade practices. Therefore, it's imperative to discern your ethical parameters before selecting your SRI avenues.

# 8.2. Locating Suitable Investment Opportunities

Finding appropriate investment opportunities that blend profitability with ethical adherence is another task. Not all companies that present themselves as 'ethical' or 'sustainable' live up to their claims. Cases of 'greenwashing' - where companies misrepresent their environmental impact - are not unheard of. Thus, due diligence is non-negotiable for a successful SRI strategy.

Investors can scout for opportunities by regularly reading reports on corporate social responsibility, sustainability, and ESG performance of potential investee companies. They can also collaborate with investment professionals and advisors specialising in SRI. Above all, understanding corporate governance structures and their approach towards ESG issues can shed light on companies that are genuinely socially responsible.

# 8.3. Balancing Profitability and Ethical Commitment

Another challenge is maintaining a balance between profitability and commitment to ethical norms. While many socially responsible investments have demonstrated strong returns, it's not guaranteed. It might involve investments in smaller or emerging market companies with novel technologies or less established business models, increasing the risk exposure.

However, several studies have shown that high ESG-rated companies tend to exhibit solid operational performance and are often financially stable. Therefore, investors must understand the business model and potential financial performance while considering SRI.

# 8.4. Adjusting to Regulatory Frameworks and Policies

Finally, adjusting to dynamic regulatory environments can be demanding. Policies and regulations around ESG factors can change rapidly, impacting the cost structure and profitability of businesses.

Investors should stay abreast of the latest regulatory changes impacting their investments, and align their SRI strategy accordingly. They could also involve policy advisory services to comprehend any complex regulations and their future implications.

# 8.5. Mitigation Techniques

Effectively overcoming the challenges in SRI necessitates a multipronged approach. Here's a rundown of some proven strategies.

Developing a strong understanding of SRI landscapes and concepts is the first step. Clarify your ethical and financial objectives, gain familiarity with common terms and principles, and understand how they apply to your potential investments. In-depth knowledge arms you not only with the ability to make well-informed decisions, but also strengthens your resilience against potential setbacks.

Engaging industry experts and advisors can help to locate suitable investment opportunities. These professionals have insights into responsible companies and can help identify credible and profitable options that align with your values.

Strike a balance between profitability and ethical commitment by diversifying your investment portfolio. Combining higher-risk, higher-potential SRI with lower-risk options can help tame volatility and smooth out returns. Consider a mix of direct investments, mutual funds, index funds, and bonds for a balanced portfolio.

Lastly, stay attuned to regulatory changes and understand how they impact your investments. Use technology to your advantage. Many digital platforms provide real-time updates on policy alterations and their potential ramifications on different sectors.

In conclusion, while the path to SRI might seem strewn with challenges initially, strategic planning, dedicated learning, and continuous engagement can transform these very obstacles into opportunities. Let's embark on this journey of making our wealth creation synonymous with societal well-being. Stay tuned for our next chapter, where we delve deeper into the exciting world of ESG metrics and their implications for your SRI strategy.

# Chapter 9. Case Studies: Successful Socially Responsible Investors

In examining the realm of Socially Responsible Investing (SRI), one can glean valuable insights from the experiences of those who have navigated the field successfully. This chapter contains detailed case studies of successful socially responsible investors, their strategies, and the impact they have made.

## 9.1. Sarah's Journey: From Skeptic to SRI Champion

Sarah was an investment manager at a prestigious finance firm in New York City. Although she was aware of SRI, she initially viewed it with skepticism, believing it to be more of a feel-good initiative than a financially sound strategy.

Sarah's perspective shifted when she attended a talk by a seasoned SRI specialist, who highlighted how SRI strategies could align with market performance. She decided to dedicate a small portion of her personal portfolio to SRI as an experiment, choosing environment-focused firms.

As she dug deeper into the companies' operations, she was impressed with their commitment to responsible supply chain management and renewable energy. Contrary to her initial skepticism, her SRI portfolio performanced on par with her traditional investments, leading her to increase her SRI allocation.

One notable success was her investment in an organic food chain that had broken ground in sustainable agriculture. The company gained substantial traction and was eventually acquired by a prominent multinational, providing a significant return.

Sarah had become an SRI champion, having seen firsthand how the power of the purse can effect change while also generating returns. Today, she leads her firm's SRI division, educating clients about the potential of this ethical investment strategy.

## 9.2. The Emmaus Credit Union: Community Values Through Investment

The Emmaus Credit Union is a community-oriented financial institution that serves a small town in the heartland of America. Traditional investing models didn't resonate with its members, many of whom were farmers and small business owners with deep ties to the land and their community.

Thus, the Credit Union developed a unique SRI strategy. They chose to invest in companies consistent with the values held by their community, such as sustainable farming practices, local job creation initiatives, and businesses that provided essential services to rural areas.

One major success came from an investment in a local wind farm project. The initiative not only created local jobs but also sold its generated power back into the grid, providing an ongoing return on the investment.

The Credit Union's SRI portfolio has become a cornerstone of its financial performance. By investing in alignment with their members' values, they have strengthened their community ties while also securing their financial future.

## 9.3. Silicon Valley Startup: Tech Meets SRI

What happens when a group of passionate, tech-savvy entrepreneurs decides to launch a firm founded on SRI principles? A case study of one such Silicon Valley startup offers some answers.

The startup started by creating a digital platform making it easy for individuals to invest in socially responsible companies. They utilized AI algorithms to identify and suggest companies that performed well financially and upheld ESG (Environmental, Social, and Governance) principles.

Start-up's portfolio included disruptors in renewable energy, sustainable agriculture, and equitable healthcare. Their first year returns outpaced several prominent tech indexes – a testament to the potential of SRI-focused financial strategies combined with innovative tech.

An entire spectrum of investors, from millennials to more seasoned individuals, gathered around the start-up's cause. Their effective marrying of tech and SRI allowed them to scale rapidly, and today, they stand as a beacon in their niche market, illustrating how innovative tech can power SRI.

These cases illustrate the success that can come from different strategies in socially responsible investing. They show that SRI is more than a trend or feel-good initiative. It represents a viable and financially sound investment strategy that can align with both the values of investors and the prosperity of the community. The ability to generate positive social impacts along with financial gains makes socially responsible investing a powerful tool for today's conscious investors.

# Chapter 10. Measurement and Evaluation of Social Impact Investments

The road to making successful social impact investments traverses a critical juncture - the systematic measurement and evaluation of the social impact generated by these investments. It's like learning a new language, a new set of metrics to gauge the value generated beyond just profit, to comprehend the social and environmental reverberations of your investments. This in-depth discussion will throw light on the rationale, methodology, and use cases of assessing the impact of socially responsible investments.

## 10.1. The Rationale Behind Social Impact Measurement

The impetus to measure the social impact of investments is manifold. At the heart of it lies the desire to assess whether the socio-environmental objectives of the investments are being met. It also provides a comparative framework to judiciously allocate resources and draw out the nuanced differences between multiple investment options, each promising a different kind of social impact. Furthermore, it facilitates communication about the investment's mission and impact, helping garner support from stakeholders.

Take, for example, a social enterprise focused on reducing greenhouse gas emissions. Investors are not just interested in its forecasted financial return, but also the actual amount of emissions averted as a result of its operations. Such a quantitative measurement offers insight into the investment's impact and helps investors make informed decisions.

# 10.2. The Methodology of Social Impact Evaluation

The evaluation of social impact is an intricate process which commences with defining the desired outcome. Thereafter, relevant indicators are identified and baseline data for these indicators is gathered. As investments unfold, data is systematically collected and compared against the baseline. Impact is thereby determined by the difference evident in the quality of life, environment, or the societal condition the investment aims to better.

Let's delve into these steps:

1. **Identify Desired Outcome**: The first step involves crystallizing what specific social or environmental outcome the investment seeks to enhance.

2. **Define Key Indicators**: Indicators should be specific and measurable, encapsulating both the breadth and depth of the desired outcome.

3. **Baseline Data Collection**: Baseline data provides a crucial point of reference, giving a picture of conditions before the investment's influence.

4. **Outcome Data Collection**: This is a continuous process throughout the lifetime of the investment. Rigorous monitoring ensures real-time adjustments and accountability.

5. **Comparative Analysis**: The outcome data is compared against the baseline to reveal the difference caused by the intervention, which represents the social impact.

# 10.3. Impact Measurement Frameworks

Several bespoke and standardized frameworks are available to guide investors in evaluating the social impact of their investments. A few notable ones are:

1. **Theory of Change (ToC)**: A comprehensive plan representing how and why a desired change is expected to happen due to an intervention.

2. **Logic Model**: Depicting in a schematic way the expected evolvement from the resources utilized (inputs) to the resulting impact.

3. **Social Return On Investment (SROI)**: An approach that quantifies social and environmental impact into monetary values.

4. **IRIS (Impact Reporting and Investment Standards)**: A catalog of generally-accepted performance metrics by the Global Impact Investing Network (GIIN).

Each of these frameworks carry their own pros and cons, and the decision to adopt a certain framework will rely on the unique requirements of the investment under scrutiny.

# 10.4. Challenges & Solutions in Impact Evaluation

Despite the wealth of measuring frameworks, the practice of social impact measurement is not without limitations. Challenges arise due to factors like intangibility of certain impacts, lack of standardization in metrics, complexity of social problems targeted, and the time delay in achieving concrete results.

The way forward lies in collaborative efforts to standardize social impact metrics, awareness creation, offering technical assistance to investors, and leveraging technology to automate data collection and tracking. Thought leaders in the sphere are already pioneering initiatives to mitigate these challenges, aiding investors to look beyond the balance sheet and appraise the immeasurable better.

Despite the complexities associated, impact measurement is an indispensable element of socially responsible investing. As the drumbeat for socially responsible investing increases its tempo, this guide to the measurement and evaluation of social impact investments provides a sturdy starting point. With consistent practice and refinement, investors can unearth a more comprehensive picture of their capital's influence, laying the groundwork for an optimal mix of fiscal returns and societal betterment.

# Chapter 11. Charting Your Course: A Practical Guide to Start Investing Socially

In the rapidly evolving financial landscape, socially responsible investing (SRI) has emerged as a beacon guiding investors towards the unexplored synergies between wealth creation and core ethical values. As navigators on this thrilling expedition, our primary task is to chart a strategic course for integrating social responsibility into your investment portfolio. With this comprehensive guide, we endeavor to demystify the essential building blocks of SRI and arm you with practical steps to kick-start your journey towards fiscally and ethically sound investing.

## 11.1. Understanding Socially Responsible Investing

Socially responsible investing represents an investment strategy that considers financial returns and social or environmental impact. But before embarking on your journey, it is crucial to understand the three pillars of SRI: Environment, Social, and Governance (ESG). Each plays a critical role in evaluating the ethical and fiscal health of the companies you invest in.

**Environment** relates to a company's interaction with the natural world. This includes its carbon footprint, waste management, resource conservation, and overall environmental stewardship.

**Social** refers to a company's relationship with its employees, suppliers, customers, and the communities where it operates. Factors such as labor practices, data protection and privacy, human rights, and community impact fall under this umbrella.

**Governance** deals with a company's leadership, executive pay, audits and internal controls, shareholder rights, and transparency.

# 11.2. Initiating Your Socially Responsible Investment Journey

Once you grasp what SRI entails, the next step forms your investment strategy. Start with introspection - identifying your primary financial objectives and ethical concerns. Establish the weightage of each ESG factor based on your personal values and the kind of social change you wish to bring about.

The next step is to research and identify potential investment opportunities that align with your defined strategy. There are several resources available to help with this task, including sustainability ratings by agencies like Sustainalytics or MSCI's ESG ratings. Additionally, consult financial advisors who specialize in SRI.

# 11.3. Diversify Your SRI Portfolio

For any sound investment strategy, diversification is key. In SRI, it allows a balanced approach towards meeting your financial objectives and social responsibility commitments. To diversify:

- Mix Assets: Consider a combination of assets, such as stocks, bonds, and funds, from different sectors.

- Go Global: Expand your geographical scope. Participate in international markets to support global progress towards environmental and social responsibility.

- Engage in Different Strategies: Blend various SRI methods - negative screening (avoiding harmful sectors), positive screening (seeking out beneficial sectors), impact investing (aiming for specific social outcomes), and shareholder activism (exerting influence for change).

# 11.4. Implementing SRI: The Practical Steps

Armed with the knowledge of SRI and a strategy in place, it's time to implement your plan.

1. Open An Investment Account: Start by opening a brokerage account if you don't have one. If you already have an account, check if the brokerage offers SRI options.

2. Start Small: Invest a small amount initially to familiarize yourself with SRI process. Keep track of the performance and impact of your investment.

3. Regular Evaluation: Regularly evaluate and adjust your portfolio in response to its performance, evolving financial objectives, or shifting social values.

# 11.5. Measuring the Impact of Your SRI Portfolio

The final step is to measure the impact of your SRI portfolio. Two key factors to gauge are financial performance and sustainable impact. Both allow you to ascertain whether your portfolio is meeting its goals: generating returns and driving social change.

Many rating systems and impact measurement tools are available to evaluate SRI portfolios. These metrics are becoming more sophisticated and accurate, enabling investors to evaluate the direct social or environmental consequences of their investments.

With these practical steps, you're ready to embark on your SRI journey. Remember, investing is a marathon, not a sprint. Patience and consistency are as important as strategy and diversification. Continue learning, stay informed about new developments, and keep refining your strategy. Socially responsible investing is not just a trend; it's becoming the new heart of investing. It's not just about wealth creation, but also about paving the way for a sustainable and just future.